I'm Over It Now

Anita Delande

iUniverse, Inc.
Bloomington

The views expressed in this work are solely those of the author and do not necessarily reflect the views of the publisher, and the publisher hereby disclaims any responsibility for them.

iUniverse books may be ordered through booksellers or by contacting:

iUniverse
1663 Liberty Drive
Bloomington, IN 47403
www.iuniverse.com
1-800-Authors (1-800-288-4677)

Because of the dynamic nature of the Internet, any Web addresses or links contained in this book may have changed since publication and may no longer be valid.

ISBN: 978-1-4502-6864-6 (sc)
ISBN: 978-1-4502-6865-3 (ebk)

Printed in the United States of America

iUniverse rev. date: 12/4/2010

For My Sons and Grandchildren
And My Nephew Who Started Me On This Journey To Healing

Chapter One

The Beginning

It was Christmas morning, 2008 and I couldn't sleep all night. Thoughts of writing my story were spinning around in my head. The night prior while attending my nephew's Christmas Eve Birthday party he told me he had a dream about me, he said I'm speaking to a group of young women at a Woman's conference. He told me that I have a story to tell and a lot of young and older women are waiting to hear it. I knew then that God is trying to speak to me through my Nephew. He just couldn't get through to me because there's always a cloud of marijuana around me.

I'm hoping that by writing down my story will be a healing experience for me. I've been putting a band-aid on a wound that's been bleeding for too many years, which has never healed and never stop hurting. I've told my older sister that I need to write this story for myself and for others young and older women who have gone through the same things and survived. Part of me wants to keep silent but part of me wants to step out on faith, be brave and courageous and tell my story. I think I have to listen to the voice inside of me, it's telling me to step out on faith and I think that voice that is pushing me is the voice of God. I've talked to my sisters and brothers about how they feel about me writing this book and they all said they're ok with it. If it will help me to heal to go for it but I'm still worried that when they see the words in writing and because of some of the things I've written they might change their mind.

My story should have come out years ago, but until my nephew said those words to me I never thought or even imagined that writing about it would help me to get over it and feel better about myself. So many times I wanted to talk to my mother and my grandmother about what happened to me and my baby sister, unfortunately they both passed away without ever giving me an explanation for why they didn't do anything to protect us. It's been very hard for me to deal with the fact that the two people who are supposed to protect you from harm, your parents are the two people who betrayed you.

The bible says to honor your mother and father but how can I do that? I pray to God all the time to help me not to hate my mother or my grandmother. I do love them and try not to judge them but I do hate my father. Even though I know I have to forgive him for myself and not him. My only consolation is that I know he will burn in hell one day. Some of his suffering has already started because he lives alone in Florida and my sisters and brothers really don't care about him except for my older sister. The rest of us just tolerate him and I am just waiting for him to pass away.

Chapter Two

Dysfunctional Family

I guess I should start at the beginning when I was born. I am the second daughter of eight children born with blonde hair and blue eyes. That was the first obstacle I had to overcome all my life but certainly more as a child. My mom's background is African American and Cuban and my father's background is African American, Indian and White. My great grandmother on my father's side was half white. Her father was white and she had blue eyes and blonde kinky hair just like me. I was named after her, and when I saw pictures of her I did resemble her except her hair was kinkier than mine.

All my life thru my school years and at all my jobs they thought I was White. Looking like I was White was always a battle for me. Maybe battle is the wrong word to use because I don't usually fight. Maybe struggle would be a better word to use. I never wanted to pass for White, inside I feel just as Black as Sidney Poiter, but people only see my blonde hair, blue eyes and light skin. Children and teens can be so cruel, always calling me names. I had fights occasionally when my rage couldn't be stifled anymore. Not just from this issue but because of what I was going through also.

I was born in Lincoln Hospital in the Bronx and raised there near Crotona Park until the seventh grade when we moved to Long Island. I had Uncles and Aunts and lots of cousins who also lived in the Bronx and my grandmother and grandfather on my mother's side lived close by.

They played a very important role in my earlier years as far as providing extras for me and my sisters and brothers because we were poor. My father was an alcoholic who hardly worked and my mom didn't work at that time, staying home taking care of her children.

My paternal grandmother lived in Long Island, she was my heart and I loved her dearly. My paternal grandfather lived in Harlem we saw him occasionally, but he was not involved in our lives that much. I remember he was a very handsome Indian looking man with straight black hair. He was never mean to us, but nothing like my grandfather on my mom's side, who was kind, funny, and generous to us. He was totally opposite to my grandmother who was a beautiful light skinned woman with brown hair, she was very generous to us but sometimes mean to me. I often thought she hated me because of what my father did to me, like she felt it was my fault. I wondered and still do to this day why she never helped me.

My mother's father was not her biological father because her real father passed away when she was a child. My mother loved her stepfather as a real father and so did all of her children. My mom's real father was a Cuban man who was a merchant marine and was away from my mother all the time. She said he would bring her gifts from all the ports he went to. My mom was an only child, raised by her grandmother. She told us she was very lonely as a child and that's why she wanted a lot of children.

She had five beautiful daughters in a row and then three sons in a row. My sister died when she was eight years old from rheumatic heart fever and my baby brother died as an infant right after my mom had him at home. That's one day I'll never forget, my mom was laying in the bed, blood on the sheets, the ambulance coming and taking her and the baby to the hospital. All of us standing around crying wondering what was going on and why were they taking our mother and new baby brother away. My mother came home a few days later but not my baby brother. I don't think we had a funeral for him, but just laid him to rest with my sister. We lived in Long Island when that happened, so I guess I was about 13 years old but I'm jumping ahead too fast.

I grew up in the South Bronx in a fairly decent neighborhood near Crotona Park with my mother and father and my sisters. We lived in a semi-basement two bedroom apartment near the park. We would go to the park everyday weather permitting. It was a huge park with several playgrounds, lots of hills to skate on and a pool that we would go to everyday in the summer. We lived next door to a candy store but they also sold milk and bread and the woman who owned the store would let my mom have things on credit when she didn't have any money to pay for it.

We had two sets of bunk beds in our bedroom and my older sister and I used to fight a lot and my other sisters would sit on the top bunk and watch us. My favorite uncle lived at the end of the block in another apartment building. My mother's mother lived close by in a very nice apartment building with a huge courtyard outside, a beautiful lobby inside and an elevator.

My father's mother worked for a black doctor who lived two blocks away in a beautiful apartment. She would take me there to help her clean his apartment and he was supposed to be my "godfather". He would give my grandmother money to buy clothes or things for me and give me a couple of dollars sometimes to buy candy for myself. I remember he had an accent because he was "West Indian" as my grandmother would say. He was always nice to me and my grandmother and became blind in his old age. My grandmother still continued to take care of him for many years, cleaning his house and cooking for him.

My little sister became ill with rheumatic heart fever and was in and out of the hospital a lot during that time. It seemed like one day she was fine and the next day she was in the hospital. She was named after my mother's mother and when she became sick and eventually passed away my grandmother was distraught. My older sister was also her favorite grandchild and she never felt bad about letting the rest of us know that. She drank often and would always fight with my grandfather when she got drunk, but I guess he loved her and put up with it.

I remember one Christmas Eve sneaking and watching them bring in all our presents from our bedroom door but by the end of the night my grandmother was drunk, arguing and fighting with my grandfather and picking up a TV antenna and hitting him in the head with it. My grandfather just walked out the front door to get away from her looking so hurt. When my grandmother didn't drink she took care of my grandfather, cooked great meals and kept an immaculate apartment.

They both worked for Revlon perfume company up in Yonkers until they both retired.

****

I haven't written anything for about three months. I know I should be writing, even as a journal, jotting down my feelings over the past months. I've been living with my sister for a while, then with my niece. Trying to look for a second job to save up money to get my own place but there are no jobs out there because of the recession. I feel lucky to have my job as a counselor with children but it doesn't pay too much and most of the time I worked a second job.

I finally was able to move with my income tax return to my own apartment. I've been very depressed lately feeling awful about the way my life has turned out. I'll be sixty years old soon and I have no permanent home, no really good job to be able to take care of myself financially. All my sisters and brothers have their own homes, and pretty good lives, but I can't seem to get my life together and to stop smoking and being addicted to marijuana.

I decided to read my bible for encouragement to finish this book. When I opened it the first thing I saw was a picture of my mother-in-law smiling at me. I loved her so much like my own mother from the first moment we met. I could hear her voice telling me to read Psalms this morning. I started to read Psalms 19, one of the verses says "oh that now my words were written down, oh that in a book they were even inscribed". So I have decided to write these words from my heart again not so much as a book but as a journal.

My granddaughter and I watched Tyler Perry's movie "Ma'Dea Goes to Jail" last night and she says you can't blame your mother or your father, grandfather, aunt, uncle for your own life. I hope it's not too late to leave some kind of legacy for my sons and grandchildren. I feel so much less than my sisters and brothers almost like the black sheep of the family because I have really nothing accomplished or to show for my almost sixty years of life on this earth.

Chapter Three

Flee Out The Window

I question God all the time and ask him why he's made my life so hard. But in reality I've made so many mistakes and bad decisions in my life, but why? Because of something that started to happen to me when I was five years old, and I can't get over it. I know I was about five years old because when my mother would take my sister to school he would put me in their bed and molest me while she was gone. How do you get over the fact that the two people, your parents, who are supposed to protect you and take care of you are the two people who betrayed you? My father sexually abused me from the age of five until I was in the fifth grade and my mother caught him. She saw him with her own two eyes and still took him back when I was in the seventh grade.

I'll never forget that day she actually caught him. I think she was suspicious for a while but maybe didn't want to believe it or face it. Most of the time he would abuse me when had been drinking or was already drunk, that day he sent her to the store but she only pretended to go and she came back and caught him. They started to fight and my mother kept screaming at him, "why"? My grandmother was at the front door, we lived in an apartment on the ground floor, she broke the window and climbed in but my father jumped out the kitchen window and ran. I truly believe that my grandmother would have killed my father that day.

I never saw him again after that day until I was graduating from the sixth grade. My mother had brought me a beautiful white dress and shoes and even though I was still in the tomboy stage I loved them. My mother and grandmother came and then he showed up with a bunch of red roses in his hand from the house he had brought in Long Island. That was supposed to erase what he did to me and I was supposed to forgive and forget. I hated him being there and I hated my mother for allowing him to come and ruin my day. I went home and took off the dress and went to the park and stayed there all day, scared he would still be there when I got home, but he wasn't.

I often wondered and still do why my mother and grandmother didn't have him arrested? I guess in those days and still even today it's such a taboo subject that it just gets swept under the rug and you don't speak about it. I guess I was supposed to just forget about it, I never received any counseling or kind words from my mother or grandmother. Little did I know my mom would reunite with him and move us from the Bronx to Long Island.

There were many bad memories of my father when we lived in the Bronx but some really stand out in my head. One time when my mother wouldn't let him the apartment because he was drunk he took a street garbage can and threw it into the front window. I remember him banging on the door for a long time, yelling and screaming for her to open it. She stood on the inside of the door holding the lock tight telling him to go away. We were all up crying and scared and then finally hearing the loud crash of the window breaking and the garbage can coming in and landing on the living room floor. Some neighbors must have called my uncle or the police because they came and he ran.

Once when they were separated after jumping out of the window he hid in the hallway because he thought she was out with another man and hit her in the head with a fishing rod. She came in the apartment still stunned and her head was bleeding. My uncle came and took her to the hospital to have stitches in her head. My cousin told me years later that my uncle looked for him with a gun that night and probably would have killed him if he had found him.

During the time they were separated my little sister got very sick from rheumatic heart fever and she passed away. I remember my uncle (My grandmothers brother) finding me and my sisters playing on our block. He looked like he was upset about something, not smiling and playing with us like usual. We went inside to the apartment and my mother told us that our sister had died. I remember crying and wanting to see her because I didn't believe it. I stayed in my room crying most of the time, watching all of our family members coming to our house, drinking and laughing, bringing all kinds of food and acting like it was a party. I wanted to go and yell at them to all get out, stop laughing and drinking because my sister had just died.

It wasn't until many years later that I understood that in the black culture we celebrate the person's life. I remember that I told my uncle that I wanted all those people to get out. He was everything to me that a father should've been and I knew he would do what I asked him to do, he never told me no about anything. Instead of helping me put them out he just picked me up and held me in his arms for a long time. I finally calmed down and stopped crying because I felt so safe and loved in his arms. Nobody has ever made me feel like that again and probably never will.

I loved my uncle and aunt and their daughters, my older cousins so very much. They lived in the Bronx and every weekend and summer I would stay with them so I could get away from my house and my father. If I didn't have them in my life to make me feel loved and safe I don't know how I would have survived the abuse. They always lived close by but I mostly remember when they lived in the projects in the Bronx.

Saturday mornings we would first go to the butcher and my aunt would buy all her meat for the week. Then we would go to the record shop and my cousins would buy all the latest 45's and my uncle had his favorites too. Then we would go back to the apartment and listen to the records all day and evening. He would pick up a little pint of his favorite drink for him and my aunt to share. Then on Sundays he would eat ice pops all day long while she made a great Sunday dinner for all of us to eat. I always wished He could be my father and I could stay there with them forever.

During the week I could hardly wait for five o'clock to come because that's when he came home from work. He was never mean or evil and grouchy like my father. When he walked into the apartment he'd kiss my aunt and cousins, his daughters and then pick up my sister and I and say he was going to throw us up 'the golden stairs". We never knew what the golden stairs were but we loved it when he would throw us up into the air. I would stand at the window and wait for him to get off the train in front of the projects and start walking up the hill to get home.

I also remember my mother having five beautiful girl cousins who would come to our house every Sunday after they came from church. They would spend the day with us and they were always dressed up with their high heels on looking so pretty. I admired them and wanted to be just like them when I grew up. They would always bring us something, either candy or some fruit. When they grew up they brought a house in Philadelphia and we would go and spend the summers with them. They brought us new clothes and give us an allowance and for two months I would be happy, safe and loved. Two of them went away into a convent to be nuns and I remember missing them very much. I was too young then to understand what a convent was or what it meant to become a nun.

Their father was my grandmother's brother and was an alcoholic as well, and didn't take care of his family either. They told me many years later they often went to bed hungry because they had no food. Their mother stayed with their father until they were grown and brought the house in Philadelphia and moved her to their new house. She died a little while after they moved to Philadelphia. She was sweet, kind and loving just like my mother but didn't have what it takes to leave. When my mother was sick with cancer they came to the hospital almost every day to help take care of her. They wouldn't stay at my mother's house because they didn't like my father so they stayed with me. The oldest one told me she knew about what my father did to me but she never said anything because of my mother and she was sorry she never spoke up. I told her it was ok I wasn't mad or angry but I couldn't help thinking another person who knew what was happening to me that didn't help me.

****

That's the key word "survived". I survived but how did I survive. What state of mind am I in and what kind of life have I made for myself and my sons? At 59 years of age I have to work two jobs just to make it. I've made wrong decisions at every important turn in my life and it's probably because I've smoked marijuana since I was in the 12th grade. And since my husband sold weed most of the time it was always accessible.

That's where all your money goes to keep your supply going and eventually you realize you're addicted to it. Not physically like heroin, you won't get sick, but your mind will keep telling you, you have to have it. You start your morning off with it, with your cup of coffee and you end your day with it at night before you go to bed to help you sleep. When I count up the money I have spent I understand why I don't have a lot of "things", and the fact that my husband is dead. It's really hard when you don't have a partner to help you, also it's very lonely. He's been dead now for 17 years now and I've never remarried. Not because I don't want to but again because of bad choices.

I tried to turn my life around after he died, going back to college full time, being lucky enough to work in the Dean's office and receiving social security benefits for my sons. My husband was very abusive and started slapping me before we were even married in High school. I went from an abusive father to an abusive husband. I had very low self esteem because I thought no one would want to marry me after what my father had done.

Chapter Four

Tries to Abuse Again

I guess I jumped ahead again and forgot to write that yes, my mother got back with my father and moved us to Long Island when I was in the seventh grade. I couldn't believe that my mother was going to make us live with him again. My grandmother begged my mother not to go back to him but I guess my mother believed she was doing the best for us getting us out of the Bronx. My father brought a house and brainwashed my mother that he had changed. But he hadn't changed at all or stopped drinking. He was the same no good bastard he always was.

Soon after we moved to Long Island he called me into the house, my mother had gone to the store and left me there by myself. I was scared because he would always call my name to come to him before he abused me. I was outside sitting on the front lawn playing cards by myself which is what I did most of the time. Why would she go and leave me there knowing already what he had done to me?

This is what has plagued me all my life wondering why she would give him the opportunity to hurt me again. Did she leave knowing what he would do to me? Was she afraid of him or did she not love me anymore? Did she hate me? I'll never be able to know why because she left us at age 67 and I never had the courage to ask her, so I can only wonder.

I know my mom had a rough life growing up without her father and my grandmother was off living her life, letting my mom be raised by her mother. At one point in her life my grandmother was a lesbian. I didn't find out about that until I was grown and saw pictures of my grandmother with her lover. I often wondered if my mother had been abused herself as a child. She was very claustrophobic and said it was because her uncle had locked her in a closet when she was a little girl.

Why didn't she take me with her that day. When I came into the house he was in the bedroom and told me to get on the bed. I told him no and if he touched me again I was going to tell my uncle and he would kill him which is what I had wanted for years. He was surprised and shocked but not stupid, he knew his abusing me was over. He told me if I ever said anything he would kill my mother and brothers and sisters and burn the house down. Then he said something bad might happen to me. I ran out of the house and ran and ran until I was far away from the house.

Soon after that I don't know exactly when he started abusing my baby sister. I never really found out until she was in high school. I felt horrible, and guilty and I still do because I could have saved her if only I had said something or told my uncle like I threatened to do. I could have protected her and my brother because he could have died the night my father stabbed him. I have to live with that everyday of my life.

Chapter Five

Life On Long Island

After that day I constantly thought of ways of killing my father and burying him in the backyard. But who would I get to help me, I would need an accomplice. My older sister would never help me because in spite of the horrible father he was she still loved him and still does to this day. I thought of asking my cousins or my uncle, they knew what a bastard he was but how could I put that sin on their souls? They would be an accomplice to murder and go to jail and so would I. Our lives would be ruined so all I did was pray to God that he would take him out of our lives forever and stay away from home as much as possible. This made it easy for him to prey on my baby sister because my mother started to work at night.

The house we lived in was very small only 2 bedrooms, but it also had a small summer house with no heat, just one big room and a large screened porch. When relatives or my fathers friends came out from the city they would stay there. The other house was a small one bedroom cottage with heat, a small kitchen and bathroom and a living room. My father's brother and his wife lived there for a while. They were always fighting and arguing all the time, my uncle was also an alcoholic.

My fathers friends from the Bronx came out often to Barbeques and my grandfather would come out from Harlem to go fishing with my father. My father had chickens, small pigs and one time a goat that they killed and Barbequed in the backyard. When the pigs got loose my father would make us go out in the snow and cold and catch them. We also had to drag the big garbage cans out to the front of the house on garbage day because he was too lazy to do it himself.

On Sundays my mother would go get a chicken, wring its neck. pluck its feathers and fry it or make chicken and dumplings for dinner. On those nights I usually had cheerios for dinner if we had any. We took care of the goat like it was a pet then had to watch my father and his friends kill it, butcher it, cut it up and eat it.

He was often mean and cruel to us for no reason. Once my younger brothers were born he turned the basement into two bedrooms for us. It was a very cheap job and it was dark and gloomy and always smelled just like a basement. My father never worked and we were on welfare most of the time until my mother started working. We would get the welfare peanut butter, cheese, dried eggs, etc. Many nights we ate beans and rice or chicken hearts and rice with biscuits or cornbread of we had cornmeal or flour.

We never had clothes like the other kids at school and usually one pair of shoes, or second hand clothes that my mother got from the Salvation Army or the "grab bag" as we used to call it. I used to wash my panties out every night by hand to make sure I had clean underwear to wear. I still do that to this day out of habit and my sons used to make fun of me until I told them why I did it. They can't imagine being that poor. We never had fresh fruit or vegetables, only in the summer when they were cheaper. My mother would take us to the Farmers Market nearby and buy us a slice of pizza if she had the money. We occasionally had cakes or pies because there was a huge bakery outlet close by that sold things at a discount. My father would take the good stuff and give us the old or broken cakes but we were happy to have the cakes or pies even if they were old or broken into pieces.

I stayed at my uncle's house or my grandmothers, my father's mother, who also lived in Long Island. She was everything to me and I loved to be in her presence. She was warm, funny, loving and taught me things like how to be a lady, how to cook, and how to set a table. When I think of her I remember big Sunday morning breakfasts before church, Christmas time at her house. She always had lots of fancy decorations and a big Christmas tree in the living room. She always had lots of barbeques in her backyard and my great aunts would come out from the city.

One Aunt in particular who always kept her gin by her feet near the chair she was sitting in. She'd always call me and say "baby, go get your aunt some ice in her glass". Of course I would do whatever she asked me to do because I loved it when they came to visit. During the evening she'd reach into her purse and give me some money I guess for getting her ice all day, but that's not why I did it for the money, I just loved my aunts and my grandmother. She was a strong beautiful woman. Her mother was half white, and my grandmother had grayish/bluish eyes also.

She left my grandfather who used to beat her and was gone from home a lot because he was a pull man porter on the trains. She had four children with him and in those days you didn't leave your husband you just stayed and took the abuse. But she didn't and wouldn't take the beatings anymore. She worked for rich gay guys who paid her well until she met my step grandfather, remarried and had two sons with him.

He brought her a house in Long Island and she continued to work but only part time or when they would have a dinner party or for the Holidays. Sometimes she would take me with her to help out, cleaning or helping her to cook. They were very good to my grandmother and also to me, and watched me grow from a teen-ager to a young woman. They would always tell me how beautiful I was, even though I never felt very beautiful. They even offered to buy my wedding dress when I got engaged. My grandmother started to plan my wedding, even though I got pregnant and got married earlier than expected she had my reception at her house because my parents didn't do anything.

When my husband and I started to look for engagement rings my father had the audacity to get angry because he didn't ask for permission to marry me. My mother was also upset and told me that we couldn't look for rings anymore until we talked to my father. I told my mother I had no intention of asking him anything and we got into a huge fight. I left their house and stayed with my grandmother for a few days and during that time contemplated turning my father in, telling everything he had done to me and was doing to my baby sister.

I know my mother was afraid I would tell my grandmother because she called me everyday asking me to come home and finish school. I eventually went back home, we got engaged and they never brought it up again. My sister told my mother what my father was doing to her but my father said she was lying and my mother I guess believed him. How could she not believe her when she knew what he did to me? Was she that desperate to have someone love her, no matter what a rotten bastard he was?

And he was a rotten bastard I remember I watched my mother being abused and beaten by my father all the time. So many nights I would lay in my bed praying when he would come home drunk, making my mother get up and fix him something to eat. If she didn't he would yell at her and then hit her until she would get up and do it just to make him stop, until one night he hit my mother with his crutch. He had fallen off an elevated dance floor one night out a bar drinking and broke his leg. He hit her with his crutch because she wasn't fixing his food fast enough. My older sister picked up a big iron cast skillet from under the sink and hit him across the head with it, after that she called the police. He never touched my mother again after that day. I guess he knew his reign of terror was over and he realized as we all got older that we would kick his ass.

My mother finally got tired of him bullying her and being the nasty drunk that he became. One night he came home drunk like usual demanding that she get up and make him something to eat. She had just gotten home from work and was tired, it was late a little after midnight and we were watching television downstairs. I heard my father yelling at my mother and my sister and I ran upstairs to help her but she didn't need our help. She had finally gotten the nerve to knock him to the ground, since he was drunk it wasn't that hard. She was on top of him choking him and she choked him until he passed out and urinated on himself. We were yelling to my mother to stop because for a minute I think she blanked out. She finally stopped when she saw that he had urinated on himself and was out cold. She got off of him and made us go downstairs and she came with us and slept with us in our bedroom. The next day he never mentioned it but I'm sure he wondered what happened when he woke up on the floor in his own urine.

Chapter Six

Pregnant and Get Married

I got pregnant in the 12th grade and got married very quickly over the weekend when my husband came home on a weekend pass from the Air force. I met my husband when I was giving my boyfriend a birthday party. My aunt let me use her basement to throw him a party. My aunt lived in the same town as my grandmother at the time.

When he walked into the party I looked at him and was immediately attracted to him and he to me. He told me later after we were married that he thought I was an Albino at first. I quit my boyfriend the next day and started meeting him at the handball court almost every day that whole summer. My uncle, who is my grandmothers son with my step grandfather is only three years older than me had a party at my grandmother's house and he came to the party. He put hickies on my neck and I lied to my grandmother and told her that a ball hit me in the neck at the handball court. She knew I was lying, she wasn't stupid, she just said, "be careful at the handball court, maybe you shouldn't go up there so much". I was afraid she would tell my mother but she never did.

I often hung out with my uncle because my grandmother didn't worry because I was with him. We would go to parties or just hang out at different people's houses in the neighborhood. The parents didn't care and at that time the neighborhood was good so we were always safe.

My very first boyfriend was one of my uncle's friends. In fact he was the boy that I was giving the party for when I met my husband. He was sweet, kind, and crazy about me and vice versa until I met my husband that night. I should have married him, my life would have been totally different. But instead I was attracted to my husband who would turn out to be an abusive boyfriend and later an abusive boyfriend.

We always remained very close friends and would go back and forth with each other when my husband would cheat on me and we'd break up. He also had a few girlfriends, but he told me he would always love me forever even if we married other people. And it was true what he said, I did always love him and had a soft spot in my heart for him. He went away in the army to the Vietnam war and got hurt. When he came home he was in the VA Hospital in Queens. I went right away to see him. I was married by then but my husband was in the Air Force and was stationed in Guam also fighting the Vietnam War.

When I walked into the ward he was in a wheelchair with a broken leg. He still had on his pajamas and hadn't shaved yet, he looked a mess. But when he saw me his face lit up and he smiled at me and said "what are you doing here?" But inside I knew he knew I would have to come and see that he was alright. He sent me to a local store to get snacks and soda. When I came back he was dressed, shaved and waiting for me looking good.

After that day I went to see him every day. Trying hard to duck his girlfriend and his mother because they knew I was married. I lived in Queens at the time with my cousin and worked for Bell telephone Company as an information operator, When he got better he would take a cab from the hospital to my place. We would spend the night together and nobody knew except my older cousin. One night when he was out with his friends they got into a bad car accident and he was killed. I couldn't believe that he was gone from me after he made it home from the war to be killed in a car accident.

At first I was worried that I was pregnant but then I didn't care, almost hoping that I was . I didn't care about my husband or anyone else finding out. I just wanted a part of him to keep with me and his baby would be just fine. I cried in my grandmothers lap at her feet until I couldn't cry anymore, asking her why would God do such a thing. She told me not to lean on my own understanding, God always has a master plan and to have faith. I confided in her that we had been sleeping together and what would I do if I was pregnant. She told me not to worry. everything would be alright even if I was pregnant she'd always be there for me and maybe it was all God's plan. As it turned out I wasn't pregnant and my husband returned from Guam and never found out.

I eventually got pregnant again because I lost my first baby, a girl born on Halloween in 1967. I got married in May,1967 one month before graduation. I didn't know anything about birth control and in those days you couldn't go to birth control clinics and get pills without your parents consent. My husband joined the Air Force after working for Singer Sewing Company after he graduated.

When he came home on leave we had unprotected sex which led to me getting pregnant and having to get married. When I look back there were many signs that I shouldn't have married him. He cheated on me often and bullied me, slapped me, shoved me, but my self esteem was so low that I accepted it all, because who would want me after what my father had done to me.

One night he came to my town and went to a party without me, made out with a girl that I went to High School with in the backseat of his car. He put hickies all over her neck too. That Monday in school I had to face all my friends and her too. She thought I wanted to fight her over him, but I was not a fighter, just humiliated and embarrassed. We were supposed to go to the party together and I waited and waited for him, eventually I went to bed.

The first time he slapped me we had gone out with one of his friends and his girlfriend. We went out to eat and then stopped at someone's house afterwards. I later found out it was a girl he was cheating on me with. The guys went inside and we stayed in the car. They were in there for a very long time and I became very angry wondering why we were sitting in the car. When they came out I started yelling at him letting him know I knew what was going on. He slapped me hard across the face and told me to shut up. I did because I was afraid of him and embarrassed that he would hit me in front of his friend.

He dropped me off at my house and I told him not to call me that I didn't want to see him anymore. Of course he called me the next day begging me to forgive him, saying he was sorry. He blamed it on drinking too much and I eventually went back with him. After that his abuse became more and more often because I accepted it. My mother knew he was hitting me and wanted me to break up with him but I didn't think she really cared about me and I didn't listen to her.

He saved up his money from working and brought me an engagement ring. He gave it to me on Christmas Eve in 1966, and asked me to marry him. Of course I said yes because I was grateful that anyone would want to marry me and it was an escape to get out of my house and away from my father.

I moved out on graduation day, right after my graduation ceremony. I wore a pink maternity dress and since everyone knew including my teachers that I had got married in May it wasn't hard to figure out. I moved in with my cousin in Queens who had a small basement apartment in her house that was perfect for us. He was in the Air Force and was stationed at Pease Air Force upstate and would come home every weekend.

At first everything was ok and I was happy about my baby coming and to be away from my mother and fathers house. We would meet on Friday nights at a restaurant near my job and then go home together on the subway. He never hit me while I was pregnant. Sometimes we would take the train and go to his parents' house for the weekend. I loved them very much and they were good to me and treated me like their own daughter. They were very religious and Jehovah Witnesses.

My mother in law was a cook for some rich White people who owned their own horse ranch in Long Island. My mother-in-law was the best cook you will ever find anywhere. I remember she made me this huge white coconut cake for my birthday before we were even married. My grandmother and step grandfather would come over to their house if we were there on the weekend and my mother in law would cook dinner for everybody. My grandmother always told me she had the best time on those Sundays and how lucky I was to have her as a mother-in-law and I totally agreed.

I thought that since my husband came from such good parents he would be a good husband, but I was totally wrong. I was happy in those first months; I started buying baby clothes and a beautiful wooden cradle that rocked back and forth. I would go to my parents' house sometimes to see my mother and sisters and brothers.

One weekend when I was there I went into early labor, my baby wasn't supposed to come until November and she was almost a month early and had a heart defect. I only saw her for a little while before they took her to an incubator and a special hospital for children. She lived for three days and then she passed away.

I knew something was wrong when my husband walked into my hospital room. I could tell he had been crying and I asked him what was wrong never thinking that it was the baby. He told me my baby girl didn't make it. We had named her Keisha Lynn. I started to scream and cry and beg him to take me to see her, but hr wouldn't. He said she had turned blue and it was best that I didn't see her. I never got to say good-by to her and hold her in my arms again. We never had a funeral or memorial for her. My husband took care of everything while I was in the hospital. I left the hospital and went home to my apartment in Queens. I didn't want to see anyone and went straight to our bedroom and our bed and just stayed there. My husband had carefully hidden all the baby clothes and the bottles and the beautiful wooden baby cradle that I had picked out for her. She was beautiful with lots of dark curly hair and bluish/grayish eyes like mine.

My cousin came to my room as soon as I got home and let me cry in her arms until I couldn't cry anymore. She would come to my room everyday and try to get me to get out of the bed and get dressed. She took it slow and steady encouraging me, telling me that my baby was with God in heaven the best place you can be. For a while I thought if she's in heaven I want to go there to, she needs me but my cousin told me God doesn't want you yet. I never would have gotten better if it hadn't been for my cousin helping me.

She and her husband were always there for me since I was a young girl and I loved her and her sister very much.

I eventually got better and went back to work and tried to get on with my life. That would have been the perfect time for me to leave the marriage, go back to college and become a teacher like I wanted to do. But instead I stayed with him working at the phone company. He was still in the Air Force stationed in Boston, coming home on the weekends. We continued to go to Long Island on the weekends to his parents or to my sister's house.

She had gotten married and her and her husband bought a house near my mother. She had two sons one right after the other. She and her husband worked at the state hospital near by and so did my mother. My father was still an alcoholic working only occasionally. When he didn't work he stayed in his room all day long watching TV during the week and getting drunk on the week-ends.

It was during one of his week-end drunks that he and my baby brother got into a huge fight and he stabbed him. Both my brothers had joined the Army and finished their time but my older brother decided to stay in and was stationed in Germany. I know if my other brother had been there it would not have happened. I'll never know why my father stabbed him, he was drunk and I don't think he even remembered the next day. My brother won't talk about it but I think it may have been because my father touched my brother's girlfriend.

My father knows no boundaries when it comes to women and respecting them. He often tried to touch and hit on my girlfriends when they came to our house. I remember going to my parents' house that night. My aunt (my grandmother's sister) was there with my brother trying to stop the blood and waiting for the ambulance and for my mother to come home from work. My aunt and her husband had brought the house next door to my mother and moved from the Bronx. She was very upset with my father who was drunk, wanted to hurt him, but trying to help my brother who was bleeding all over the kitchen floor. The police came and an ambulance took my brother and my mother to the hospital. I kept thinking he could have killed my brother.

Why did my mother go to work from 4pm to Midnight knowing she was leaving my younger sister there with him knowing what he was capable of? Did she just want to escape from him so bad that she just didn't care about my sister and brother? My brother made it; he had to have stitches and was eventually ok. My mother stayed with him even after he almost killed my brother. Why would she stay with a man who abused your daughters and almost killed your son? Why didn't she have the courage to fight for her children and leave him?

My Aunt's husband (the one who lived next door) would often touch me when I started to develop. He would touch my ass or my breasts and then pretend it was an accident. I went to my mother several times and told her because I couldn't take it anymore, but she never did anything about it. I finally told my husband who was my boyfriend at the time. He went to him right away and told him if he ever touched me again he would beat the hell out of him.

My mother got mad at me for telling him, saying I caused a lot of trouble between her and her aunt. No regard or caring for me her own daughter. I really felt that day she didn't love me at all, and after that day she hated my husband. In spite of these things that happened I really loved my mother very much and I always told myself not to judge her or hate her because I don't know what she went through as a child or what may have happened to her.

I can't even remember my mother hugging me or comforting me when she found out what my father had done to me, or when my baby died or even after my husband died of AIDS and I had to be tested. No one came with me that day to have the results of my test given to me. There were no hugs or comforting words from her or anyone.

****

I haven't written anything in my book for a few days because when I write things down that I've never written down before it overwhelms me and I have to stop. I read my bible everyday to motivate myself to keep writing this book. Sometimes I doubt myself and the negative thoughts come saying, "you can't write this book. You don't know anything about writing a book", but I pray and just keep writing.

I want to inspire young women or girls who have been sexually abused to be the best person they can be, to do great things and know that what happened was not your fault. Today my horoscope said, "Don't underestimate your skills and talents. The greatest gift you can give is to be yourself and share your knowledge. You have a lot to offer and to just be your positive self to shower inspiration with anyone you come in contact with." I posted it on my refrigerator and I read it every day to motivate myself to write.

I also feel I can only write when I'm completely alone. My granddaughter lives with me so that makes it hard. If she sees me writing she'll ask me about it and I'm not ready for her to know about everything that has happened to me in my life yet. One day she will be old enough to understand and I will be the one to tell her and my younger granddaughter as well.

****

My husband and I were happy that first year after I lost the baby. It took me a while to get pregnant again and when I did I was very happy. He was still in the Air Force and was about to be sent back to Guam for another tour. I started going to see a psychiatrist because of what my father had done to me and because of losing my baby. I made the mistake of telling my husband what happened to me.

Years later during a really bad fight he was very cruel and said the baby died because it was probably my father's. That made me feel like he didn't believe me that it had stopped when I was in the seventh grade. After my husband went back to Guam I moved back to Long Island with my older sister and her husband. They had an extra bedroom and I got a job at the admissions office at the state psychiatric hospital where everybody worked.

I really loved working there; it was totally different from being an information operator at the phone company. I transcribed tapes from the doctors who admitted all the new patients. There was never a dull moment. I had a great supervisor who treated all of the women who worked for her in the office really special. She was kind and funny and protected us if the doctors had a complaint. She would make us Easter baskets, and on Valentines Day bring us hearts with candy in them. She always remembered our birthdays and every Friday she would cook food and bring it in for us.

The supervisors at the telephone company were mean and rude, always walking the floor and plugging in to you to listen, being critical, never saying anything good or positive. It was quite a change for me to work in an office where everyone was so nice and to have such a nice woman for a supervisor. When I found out I was pregnant again and told everyone they treated me so special. She knitted a blanket and sweater to match for the baby. They gave a big baby shower for me when the time came close for me to have my baby.

Chapter Seven

~

Goes AWOL Goes to Leavenworth

In the beginning months I was sick all the time with morning sickness but it passed after the fourth month. I was a little worried and nervous because of what happened to my baby girl but I tried not to dwell on that and be positive about the new baby. My husband was assigned to go back to Guam for another year but he went AWOL instead. The MP's came to get him from my sister's house, he ran from them thru the back yard but they got him anyway and took him back. I still think to this day that my mother called them or my older sister but I'll never know.

I went upstate to his trial which lasted a few days. He was sentenced to a year at Ft. Leavenworth for going AWOL. During that time I continued to work at the hospital and got an apartment with another one of my sisters. She also worked at the hospital, brought her first car and we also brought furniture for the apartment, dishes, curtains, etc. We even got a little puppy and I waited for my baby to come.

My sister was single and enjoying it, she went out with her friends or sometimes they would come over to the apartment and hang out. We'd make snacks and eat and laugh, they were funny and crazy. They would tell me stories about the patients at work or their dates with guys. My baby sister would come over too but then I didn't know she was getting away from my father, who was abusing her. My mother was still working 4pm to Midnight and left her there or sometimes she would go to my other sister's house to get away from him.

She told me years later that one time he came looking for her at my older sister's house. They had gone out and left the door open because in those days the neighborhood was safe. They never locked the door until they went to bed. She told me she hid in the little closet under the sink for an hour. He was drunk and just kept calling her name. He finally gave up and left. I felt so bad when she told me and angry, I wanted to kill him again like so many other times before. I should have protected her instead of leaving her there or taken her with me so she would not have to go through what I went through. I have to stop writing now for a while because the tears are flowing and I can't see or write anymore.

****

I haven't written in my book for a week but I know I have to keep writing, get it organized and finished. I've been trying to make some sort of outline to follow. Trying to put all the events and important things in my life in order but it's hard. I'm also trying to write a Gratitude Journal like Oprah suggests. Trying to find several things every day to be grateful for. I keep going back and forth in my thoughts from the past to the present. I just hope it's not too confusing to anyone who reads this.

****

My sister and I stayed in the apartment together and I waited for my baby to be born. He came in January, fat and healthy and even though my husband was in Leavenworth I was very happy. My mother was there for me and my in-laws would always check on me and come by to see if I needed anything. I was very nervous at first with my son, because I had lost my first baby but I eventually calmed down and was a good mother. It really wasn't hard because he was a happy baby thriving and smiling all the time, gaining weight and he seemed to be content.

When my baby was about three months old my husband came home. He never told me he was coming home, just came and "surprised" me as he put it. I think he was trying to catch me cheating or out with my friends. As it turned out I was at my grandmother's house with my girlfriend. When he walked through the door I was very happy to see him and surprised. He had been writing in his letters how sorry he was and how he was going to make it up to me and his son for being away and cheating on me.

While he was in prison all his belongings were sent to me. In his belongings I found letters and a picture from a girl he had been cheating on me with while he was stationed in Boston. To make matters worse she was White. My first reaction was to divorce him while he was in prison, move on and try to raise my son on my own. I was sick of the cheating, the abuse everything.

But he wore me down with his promises and his begging. My mother and my mother-in-law both were in my ear telling me I should give him another chance and to think of my son. So I let him come home to us and he moved into the apartment with me and my sister. He made no attempt to find a job, started smoking weed all the time and taking LSD staying up all night and hanging out with his friends all night. It wasn't long before he started hitting me again and he never paid any attention to our son or helped with his care.

I went back to work at the mental hospital but my supervisor knew something was wrong. I came to work often tired from getting no sleep because of my new baby or from fighting or arguing with my husband. My sister and I paid the rent and brought the food while he did nothing to contribute not even for his son, it was like those months in Leavenworth had made him not care about anything or anybody. He had no connection to anyone, not me, his son or even his parents. He never wanted to go visit them and when they came by our apartment he was never there.

Chapter Eight

Abusive Boyfriend, Pregnant, Get Married

My husband decided we should move to LA when his sister moved there. My in-laws decided to move to Phoenix, Arizona and my sister-in-law and her children moved there with them too. After a few months in Phoenix my sister-in-law left her kids with my in-laws and moved to LA. My husband thought it would be a way for us to make a fresh start.

Little did I know he was just trying to get me far away from my family? I went out there first, he was selling drugs by then and planned to make a lot of money and join us in a few months. I went to LA moved in with my sister-in-law in her apartment. She was totally wild, partying and sleeping with all kinds of men. I found a job with an insurance company and then my husband's other sister and her husband moved to LA. She kept the baby for me and I tried to save up money to get my own apartment.

I heard lots of stories from my sister about my husband driving around his girlfriends in our car. I really didn't care because I had met someone and started cheating on him. I really didn't care if he ever came to LA. He did finally show up with a suitcase full of money to impress me, which I wasn't. I kept cheating on him and one night he was waiting for me to come home, hiding in front of the apartment building. He punched me so hard in my mouth that I fell to my knees.

Anita Delande

My teeth punctured my bottom lip and my mouth was swollen and cut for a few days.

I left him after that and my sister came out to LA from NY and we got an apartment together. I stayed away from him. I was happy that my sister was there with me and she got a job at the same insurance company that I worked at. My husband wouldn't leave alone, he would drop by the apartment whenever he wanted and call me constantly to beg me to take him back. During that time I found out I was pregnant, and had an abortion. I knew it wasn't my husband's because I was too far along. He thought the baby was his and wanted me to have it but I knew that would've been a big mistake.

One night he snuck into the apartment with one of my sister's boyfriends. He had brought me a birthday cake because it was my birthday. I just came home from having the abortion and was sick, with cramps and didn't want to see him. When I told him that I had the abortion he turned the cake upside down on my dresser. I had to get my sister's boyfriend to talk to him and ask him to leave or I would call the police, he then left. I was always worried and fearful that he was following me or would try to hurt me. I wanted to get as far away from him as possible, so I moved back to New York with my older sister and her husband again.

Chapter Nine

Discover He's Abusing Younger Sister

My baby sister was a senior in High School by then and my mother was still working at the hospital from 4pm to Midnight. My sister stayed away from the house as much as she could. One day she came to my older sister's house crying and freezing cold because she had walked all the way from our house. She said my father had come up to the school and wanted her to get in the car with him. His plan was to take her home and abuse her but she was at the point that I had been and told him no. She got out of the car and walked to my sister's house. She told my mother what happened but she didn't believe her. Of course my father said she was lying.

The next day he came over to my sister's house and grabbed her by the hair and slapped her across the face. I was in the shower but when I came out she was hysterical and crying. My sister and her husband weren't there. That's another day I had the urge to kill my father and I was disgusted by my mother so bad I knew I had to leave NY again and take my baby sister too. So I waited for my sister to graduate and she and her best friend went with me back to LA and got an apartment together.

I moved in with my sister and her boyfriend and they were expecting their first baby. I stayed with them and saved up my money to get my own apartment. I started seeing a married man who also worked at the

Oil Company where I worked. I knew it was wrong but I was so crazy in love with him that I didn't care.

Every Friday night we would all go to "happy hour" after work at a local club in downtown LA. One night he gave me a ride home and that was the beginning of our affair. He was tall, handsome and always wore a suit and smelled good. He worked in the accounts receivable department and had worked his way up from the Refinery at the oil company.

When we first met he drove a green Volkswagen and then after a bout a year brought a beautiful blue Porsche, my favorite color. Being with him opened up a whole new world for me. He took me to fancy restaurants, sometimes on business trips with him, and we would drive there in his Porsche. We went skiing and he was good to me and a great lover. I started to neglect my son and spend a lot of time with him which I regret. I became so enthralled with him that I would leave him with my sister very often.

He was only about four years old but I'm sure he noticed I was gone a lot and his father wasn't around because he had gone back to New York. After I got my own apartment we spent even more time together and he was always at my apartment. Sometimes I would feel bad because I knew he was married and in my heart I knew he would never leave her and his two daughters. I think he had love for me and the sex was great but we really had no future together.

His wife had already found out about us, seeing us often at lunch time in restaurants because she worked only a few blocks away. He told me how she would find my long honey blonde hair all over his clothes and him but she never came and approached me. I don't think it was the first time he had ever cheated on her.

After I moved back to New York he came to NY on a business trip and we stayed at a New York Hotel for the week. I showed him the city, Central Park; we went to Harlem to the Schaumberg Museum and to Sylvia's restaurant for dinner. When my husband died he called me to talk and see if I needed anything, financially or emotionally. When my granddaughter was five years old I went back to LA for a visit with my sister and we spent time together again.

My husband was writing me and calling me from New York, begging me to go back together and do what was best for our son. I decided to go to New York and visit my family and see my husband to see if he had really changed at all. My son also needed to spend some time with his father. So we took a trip back to NY and stayed with my sister and her husband. They were having a few problems. My sister had caught her husband cheating and he was drinking a lot, she was also having a little fling of her own.

My husband was working at a hospital doing maintenance and seemed to be doing well for himself. My sister had a daughter since I moved to LA and her two sons were getting older. She told me when I was home that her husband had made the mistake of letting my father take her daughter to my parents' house. My mother was at work as usual and my sister freaked out when her husband told her that my father had taken her to the house.

She drove to the house as fast as she could because she knew what my father was capable of. If he would abuse his own daughters, he would abuse his granddaughter. Her daughter was only five years old at the time. My sister banged on the door but my Dad didn't come to the door right away. She kept yelling and banging on the door and he finally came and opened the door looking very guilty.

He said he had been in the back yard and didn't hear her. When she asked her daughter where they were she told her, "Grandpa took me to the basement". My sister said she knew what he was going to do or had already done and told him if he ever touched her daughter she'd kill him and stand over his grave and curse him to hell. This was the same sister who had hit him in the head with the cast iron skillet and had no fear of him.

I know he was also afraid of what my brother-in-law would do to him. I asked her why she didn't call the police and she said she wouldn't want to humiliate or embarrass our mother. So again the shit was swept under the rug and my father got away with what he had done or tried to do to his granddaughter. But that's what happens when things are hidden and kept secret. If my sister had told my brother-in-law what my father might do he would have never let his daughter go with him. I never went to my parents' house or saw my father that time I went to visit. My mother would come to my sister's house and visit and I don't think my sister even told my mother what happened.

I don't want anyone reading this book to think that I didn't love my mother. I loved her very much, she was kind, generous with a heart of gold, but she was weak when it came to my father and I think she had very low self esteem like me. I try not to judge her because I know that's wrong and I don't know still to this day what she went through as a child herself.

She sometimes spoke of an Uncle Peanut who would lock her in a closet, that's why she was very claustrophobic. He was her grandmother's brother and when she spoke of him there was sadness in her voice. I often wondered why he locked her in a closet but she never wanted to talk about it. Was it to scare her or intimidate her into doing things she didn't want to do? Was she also abused as a child? Like I said, she never wanted to talk about what happened to her or to me even when she knew she was dying from cancer.

Chapter Ten

Move to Los Angeles

My husband and I got along really well during my visit to NY and he spent almost every day with his son. I went back to LA thinking we might have a chance to make it again and I had to stop thinking of myself my son needed his father to be in his life if he was willing to change. My married friend was very happy to see me when I came back to LA, even though he knew I had spent time with my husband. He was very content to continue the same relationship we had, just seeing me on the week-ends or once or twice a week. He had no intentions of leaving his wife and daughters.

So I started to encourage my husband to come to Los Angeles so we could try to be a family. My son was five years old by then and my husband wanted us to try and have another baby. I wanted another baby too, maybe this time a little baby girl. So a few months after I came back from NY my husband moved back to LA into my apartment with me and my son. My friend wasn't happy about it but he wasn't going to leave his wife for me. I wasn't ready to give him up completely and he still wanted to keep me on the side.

So we continued to see each other. I think my husband suspected something was going on because one day when I was at work he went through all my purses and my ski jacket. He found old ski lift tickets with my friends name and address on them. He came up to my job one day at lunchtime and followed us to a restaurant. He walked in and came up to our table; my heart was in my throat because I didn't know what he was going to do. He just said, "You should have told me" and walked out. He went to my friend's house and told his wife that we were having an affair. She was very angry because he had told her that it was over between us. She put him out and he got his own apartment which made it easier for us to sneak and be together. I told my husband that I wouldn't see him anymore but I just couldn't stay away from him.

I stopped taking birth control because my husband still wanted to have another baby. Most of the time my friend and I used condoms but sometimes we didn't and when I got pregnant I wasn't sure whose baby it was. My husband was happy because he thought it was his and my friend was happy because he thought the baby might be his. He was still separated from his wife and still living in his apartment. They were thinking of getting a divorce but for me it was too little, too late. He never really wanted to leave her on his own she had put him out after finding out everything. We still continued to see each other and sleep together after I was pregnant.

One day we both took off from work and I went to his apartment and we spent the day together. I was five months pregnant then, I don't think I'll ever forget that day as long as I live. My husband called my job and they told him I wasn't in, then he called my friend's number and found out he wasn't in. He put two and two together and came to his apartment. I still to this day don't know how he knew where his apartment was but he came there and pounded on the door. I was scared, my friend wanted to call the police but I stopped him.

I finally just opened the door to leave but he pushed past me and punched my friend in the face and the eye. He followed me out of the apartment but he never touched me or hit me. He took me home and then left and went back to my friend's apartment. He broke all the windows and the windshield on my friend's new Porsche. He told me later on after several months that he also had some of his friends go and break into his apartment and rob him.

I stayed away from him after that because I was really afraid of what my husband would do to him and I was really ashamed of myself. Asking myself what kind of woman had I become to not know who the father of my baby was and to continue to sleep with someone else when I was five months pregnant. My husband tried to forget everything and show me love in spite of what I had done. He brought me a beautiful rocking chair and hand painted it with flowers and put my name on it. My second son was born and I knew as soon as I looked at him that he was my husband's baby because he looked just like his brother. My husband was happy and we tried to put everything behind us, but it didn't last.

I went back to work after three months and I would see my friend often. His wife had let him come back home and they were trying to make it work. It wasn't long before my friend and I were sneaking off from work on extended lunch hours and meeting at the hotels close by where we worked. We were very careful this time and we never got caught. My husband thought he had scared him off but he was so wrong. We continued to have an affair for the next 15 years and I just couldn't give him up. My husband had his little flings on the side too but I didn't care because I always had my friend and lover in the background. I guess you could say we had real feelings for each other maybe even love.

We moved into a new apartment in the same block that my sister lived in. My husband worked as a youth counselor and I was working, we had our two sons and we tried to make it work for a while. My baby sister had met a nice man and was about to be married. They were planning their wedding and my other sister and I were going to be bridesmaids. My mother and brothers and sister from New York were coming, also my grandparents. My baby sister had asked my grandfather to give her away and didn't want my father to come to the wedding. I was happy about her decision but afraid that my mother wouldn't come but she did. We had a really great day, a happy one, and they had planned a beautiful wedding.

Everyone stayed for about two weeks, it was nice to spend time with my mother and grandmother and it seemed like we had all put the past behind us. We took my mother and grandmother to see the play "For Colored Girls" and to the Red Onion a Mexican restaurant where we had pitchers of Margaritas. We even went to a male strip club for my sister's bachelorette party. My mom was too shy and quiet to wave her dollar bills but my grandmother had a great time, waved her dollar bills and enjoyed the show. My sister was a beautiful bride and as I watched her walk down the aisle with my grandfather I couldn't help but think she's finally getting what she deserves, a happy life with a good man. Some of the guilt I felt had gone away but I would still never get over feeling bad that I hadn't protected her.

Soon after my sisters wedding my grandmother (My father's mother) got very sick with cancer. She had come to LA to go to my sisters wedding but she was so sick when she got there she couldn't even go. She was my heart and when my mother called and told me to come ASAP if I wanted to see her alive. I left right away and went straight to my parents' house, where my uncles and aunts and all my cousins were. My mother took me to the hospital right away and when I walked into the room she was in a coma, with a breathing tube in her throat.

My father was in a chair beside her bed and he looked terrible, really sad and I guess I felt sorry for him because I know he loved his mother and so did I. We spoke briefly and then he left the room so I could be alone with her. I lay down on the bed with her, talking to her even though I didn't know if she could hear me.

Sorry that I hadn't been there close to her, sorry that I had to get so far away from her son, my father. Sorry that I hadn't been there for her when she got so sick like she had always been there for me. I stayed for a week, going to the hospital every day with my mom or my aunt. My aunt was my dad's only sister, a beautiful tall woman with a light complexion, chestnut brown hair, a great smile and flawless skin. I noticed the tension between her and my father, they never spoke and when he walked into the room she left.

When I asked her what was going on, she looked at me with tears in her eyes and said, "Your grandmother saved your fathers life because I was going to kill him". She told me that my father had molested her daughter and when she found out she went and got a gun and was going to shoot him. She said my grandmother begged her not to do it. All I could think of was another victim of my father, swept under the rug again and he got away with hurting another girl in our family. I didn't have the heart to tell her about me and my sister even though she may have already known. She was so full of grief for my grandmother and so full of hate for my father that I couldn't add to it.

Years later before she died suddenly of an aneurism I finally told her what he had done to us, her only reply was "I should have killed him when I had the chance". I told her he wasn't worth it, that God will take care of him, we hugged each other never spoke of it again. I went back to LA after a week of being with my grandmother at her death bed. She died one day after I came back home to LA. I didn't go back to NY for the funeral because I didn't really have the money to go back. Somehow I felt she knew I was there when she was alive, I had to console myself with that.

Chapter Eleven

Back To NY, Back To LA

I continued with my life in LA with my husband and two sons. I was still seeing my lover and I'm sure my husband still continued to cheat on me but I really didn't care. My sister and I lived on the same block and I was happy she was close. Our sons were in the same Little League games for basketball, football, softball and we both went to their games and had fun. We'd go to the beach every week-end together and in time we both got pregnant at the same time again.

My husband had been hinting at having another baby and I wanted to try and have a little girl too. As it turned out I had another boy and so did my sister. I had my son in October and she had a boy in December. Now we had three sons and at first everything seemed to be ok, but then my husband got laid off because of budget cuts. He stayed at home with our son taking care of him but most of the time he would drop him off to his sister and go hang out with his friends and get high.

We were both smoking marijuana then but soon after he got laid off his friends from LI moved to LA and introduced us to crack cocaine. At first he would bring it over to our apartment and get high with us for free. Crack cocaine was just coming out then as the new recreational high in the 80's and I think everybody was trying it. At first we would crumble it up and smoke it in a joint. It was the greatest high I had ever felt and we were soon getting it every week-end.

I guess I was telling myself it was ok to just smoke it with weed, not wanting to be honest with myself and admit that it was addicting. In a couple of months my husband and his friends started to smoke it in a pipe. I could tell my husband was becoming totally addicted and his friend was now charging money and my husband would sometimes spend all the money he made selling weed because he still wasn't working. I look back now and thank God for my three sons because they were the only reason I made myself stop. If I became addicted what would happen to them?

I started telling my husband not to bring it home anymore and if he did I would take my sons and go to my sister's house. He would come to my sister's house and bang on the door when he would run out of money. My sister and brother-in-law would protect me and sometimes I would have to call the police.

During that time my sister-in-law went back to college and graduated. She got a job in the Social Services Department in downtown LA and met a guy younger than she was who started her smoking crack too. She became so in love with him and addicted to crack that she left her husband and her daughter. My husband and his sister would get high together all the time after that. He now had somewhere to go to get high, usually at her apartment that she shared with her new boyfriend.

It wasn't long though before she lost her apartment and started living in cheap motels in downtown LA. Neither my husband nor his sister would ever be the same. She soon lost her job at the Social Services department too. Many nights my niece would call me crying, begging me to go with her to find her mother. I would go because I loved my sister-in-law and her boyfriend had started beating her and would take all her money. We would find her and bring her home, she would stay for a few days maybe a week but then she would go right back to him and the crack.

My husband also became more and more addicted and abusive. He would take all the money, it was so bad I had to hide the money under the carpet because if I had it in my bra he would hold me down and take it. One night I called the police and had him arrested. After that night he called one of his friends and asked him to give him a job at a cable company. He would have to go away all week and just come home on the week-ends. I was very happy to have him away because I couldn't take it anymore. But that didn't last very long because as soon as he hit LA on Thursday nights he would go and buy his crack and get high all week-end.

Chapter Twelve

No Change in NY

My sister-in-law had gotten very sick with kidney failure and was in and out of the hospital a lot. My husband must have realized he would be in the hospital soon just like her dying from his crack addiction. He begged me to go back to NY because he had convinced himself his drug addiction was because we lived in LA and he could stop if we went back to NY. So we sold most of our furniture and went back to NY. I flew back on the airplane and my husband drove back in our van with my three sons.

Nothing changed in NY. We moved into a small beat up house and he got a job in the hospital with the maintenance department and I got a job as a secretary. I was miserable being back in NY. I missed my sisters and my lover and living in LA very much. Soon after we were back in NY I knew it was a mistake and I started planning to leave him again and go back to LA. I called my sister in LA and asked her if we could come back and stay with her. Of course she said yes but we both knew it would be tight with me and my sons.

My oldest son was in High School by then and I told him I was leaving to go back to LA. We talked and we decided that he would finish out his school year and then come in the summer. Now I know it was a big mistake to leave him even though he said he would be fine. When he woke up that morning and his brothers and I were gone I hurt him a lot. I waited until my husband was at work because he worked 11pm to 7am shift. I asked my older sister and her husband to pick me up in the middle of the night and take me to the airport. I knew my husband would be furious but my need to get away from him was overwhelming, I knew he wouldn't hurt my son. My son told me later that he came into his room that morning yelling, "Where's your mother and brothers", but my son kept telling him he didn't know. He kept calling my sisters house because I'm sure he eventually figured out where I had gone. I finally talked to him after a few days, he knew why I had left again and that it was ultimately his own fault.

I stayed with my sister for a few months and got my own apartment. I was working for a Child Abuse Agency in Los Angeles and my son came to LA that summer when the school year was over. I was very happy to just be alone with my three sons even though I struggled financially because my husband would not help me or pay child support. My oldest son started to get involved in a gang; he would cut school and hang out in the streets with his friends. He started smoking marijuana and would steal it from me, and then he started to sell it.

My husband would come out to LA and visit us and sometimes we would go to NY. My son started to get into trouble and I was afraid he would end up in jail or in a juvenile Center. Eventually my husband moved back to LA because he thought he could keep our son out of trouble. We rented a house near my sister a few blocks away and for a while like before things seemed to be OK. He was constantly accusing me of going out with other men and my friend and it wasn't long before he was smoking crack again.

By then crack cocaine was kind of an epidemic in Los Angeles. It was the new fun high and everybody was doing it not realizing the consequences. A lot of my husband's friends moved to Los Angeles from Long Island, he was with them more than he was with me and our three sons. I used to spend a lot of time in church because I didn't know where else to go. I would just sit in the back and pray, no one else would be there. I didn't want to go home because I knew he would be there asking me for money or trying to steal it from me. I got my sons involved in the youth programs at church but my oldest son was still involved in a gang and acted out even more because he knew my husband was still smoking crack.

My husband went back to work at the cable company with the help of his friend. They had openings in the San Gabriel Valley on the outskirts of Los Angeles. He kept asking me to move out of LA because he thought it would help him stop getting high. We moved to the Valley to a nice 2 bedroom apartment to see if it would make a difference, but it was a big mistake. He only got worse and now he had isolated me from my sisters, which is what he wanted to do more than anything. He was smoking crack more and more, stealing money from me or tearing up the apartment to look for money when he thought I had hidden it.

One day I'll never forget, we were riding in our van, our sons were with us. We were supposed to be going to the grocery store to buy groceries but he kept asking me for money. I kept telling him no because we needed food and I wasn't going to let him spend the money on crack. He got crazed and angry the pulled over and started to hit me. I jumped out of the van and ran down the street. I didn't know where I was going maybe try to get to a phone and call my sister. He caught up with me and grabbed my blouse in the front and my bra ripping them both.

I was standing on the street with my breasts exposed and trying to cover myself. He kept hitting me and took the money as it fell from my bra. He did all this in front of my sons with no remorse. He took us back to the apartment and dropped us off and took the money to get high. That night I waited for him with my son's baseball bat. When he came in he went to our son's bedroom and slept. I waited until I knew he was asleep and tried to hit him in the head with the bat. I wanted to kill him. He woke up after I hit his shoulder and chest and thank God took the bat away from me.

Chapter Thirteen

Crack Addiction, LA and Phoenix

The next day he called his parents in Phoenix and asked them to let him come there and try to help him stop using drugs. He wanted to take our two youngest sons with him because I told him I wasn't going. I guess he felt if he could have them with him he would want to do the right thing for them. My oldest son went back to NY to stay with my older sister and finish school. I stayed in Los Angeles and moved in with my girlfriend and we shared a two bedroom apartment. I was scared to let my sons go with my husband but I knew my in-laws wouldn't let anything happen to them and they would be close by. I was still working and would send money every week to help my husband and make visits to Phoenix often.

At first he seemed to be doing OK, he got a job and an apartment close to my in-laws and tried to stay off crack. It wasn't long before he found the drug dealers and the people who got high and started using again. When I would go there on visits he would stay out all night, all kinds of drug people would come by looking for him. It got so bad I had to take my sons and go to my in-laws to stay when I was there. I finally packed them up and drove back to LA leaving him there. He eventually got evicted from the apartment and came to LA where I was staying with my girlfriend and my sons.

I had lost all love and respect for him. When I was in Phoenix for a visit I saw him pan handling in front of a 7-Eleven near their apartment.

I couldn't believe that the man I had once loved, the father of my three sons was nothing but a drugged out bum, begging people for money. He looked terrible, like a walking skeleton, with sores around his nose and mouth. I knew he was going to die soon if he didn't get help right away.

Chapter Fourteen

Final Days in New York

My oldest son was still in New York with my oldest sister and my mother was sick with breast cancer. I decided to go back to New York and try to get him some help and also be close to my mother and my son. All of his friends from LI said they would help him, some kept their word and some didn't. One of those friends got him a job at the hospital again. I worked for an aviation company and J.C. Penny part time.

My oldest son was now selling drugs and had dropped out of high school. He tried to hide his life style from me but I knew what he was doing. It wasn't long that we were back in New York before my husband started using cocaine again, smoking crack and making our lives miserable again. The good thing was that his hitting me and taking my money was over. My oldest son was now almost a grown man, one day when he started his shit my son picked him up and body slammed him hard on the ground.

After that he started to stay in the streets more and more and I was happy he stayed away. I wasn't happy about my son selling drugs and asked him to stop and go back to school but all my pleading fell on deaf ears. I guess he felt like he had to help take care of me and his brothers because his father was a lost cause.

One night when my son wasn't home my husband started to ask me for money, then begging me, he started to hit me, ripping my robe to see if I had money in my bra. I ran out of the house to a neighbor's. At first she was afraid to let me in but I kept begging her to let me call my brother or the police. She finally let me in; I called my brother and the police. By the time they came he had left but my brother went looking for him at all the local crack houses but thank God he never found him. I think my brother would have really hurt him or even killed him. I later found out he was hiding in our van in the back of the house like a coward.

Chapter Fifteen

Hospital, Death, Funeral, Breast Cancer

After that day my father really tried to be there for me and my sons. He brought me a winter coat and anytime I needed food he would tell me to go to the freezer and take what I needed. He would go and always buy groceries for us without me asking him to. He became more involved with my sons and he and my brothers would take them fishing. I started not to hate him so much and our relationship got a little better.

After that night I put my husband out for good, but he managed to get a small studio apartment. He was still using drugs and eventually caught the HIV virus. Once in a while I would take my sons to visit him because in spite of everything they still loved their father. At Christmas time we dropped off gifts to him but he never opened them.

One night I got a call from my niece in California. She said that my husband was in the hospital unconscious and on a respirator, not expected to make it. She had gotten a call from one of his friends in New York. They had been at a basketball game and he had collapsed at the game and was rushed to the hospital. They told her they didn't know how to get in touch with me. I went to the hospital right away and took my sons. He was in the IC Unit and at first they wouldn't let us in to him because in that unit they only have special visiting hours.

But after I explained to them I was his wife and I didn't know he was there they let us in. The doctors told me he was very sick and would probably not come off the respirator. I would later find out that the HIV had turned into full blown AIDS. For a month I went to the hospital twice a day and watched him die slowly. Sometimes I would get there and they wouldn't let us in because someone in the unit had died. I wondered every time they did that if it was my husband who had died.

Right before he went into the hospital my mother was diagnosed with beast cancer and had her left breast removed. She had to go through chemotherapy and was very sick from it. My youngest sister who still lived in Los Angeles got very sick after her son was born with Lupus. Her husband left her and she moved back to New York too, Even though my mother was very sick she tried to be there for both of us. My father actually shocked me taking care of my mother and my sister. I started to see him in a different light other than the bastard he always was. I hoped that he had actually changed and was sorry for the things he had done.

One day the hospital called and said that I should come right away because my husband had taken a turn for the worse. I got in my car and started to drive to the hospital but then decided to go back and get my sons to go with me. While I waited for them to get ready the hospital called and said he had already died. I sat down on the sofa and I guess I couldn't really believe he was dead. Now I had to go and tell my sons that he had already died and they weren't going to be able to say good-by.

My youngest brother was there at my house with me and he helped me tell my sons their father had passed away. They all took it pretty hard because I think they still believed we would bring him home from the hospital someday. My oldest son told me he had a dream that he saw his father in a store and they walked right past each other without acknowledging each other like they weren't father and son. That dream haunted him for a long time. He said he felt like God was trying to tell him to go say good-by to his father but he never felt like he would really die. My middle and youngest son took it hard too. They never saw their father alive after that day because I had him cremated.

I called my cousin who was like a sister to me and she and my father stood beside me while I picked out a casket and made funeral arrangements. I didn't have any life insurance for him so I had a very inexpensive memorial service for him. No one in my family came except my nephew and my youngest sister. Everyone in my family hated my husband and my mother was recovering from her cancer. My older sister and I weren't even speaking because we had gotten into a fight when he first went into the hospital.

My husband's friends were there for me and my sons and I still keep in touch with them to this day. One friend in particular who often gave me pep talks in his van. When I just couldn't walk into that hospital one more time he would tell me, "yes you can, you can do this, you have to, and I'll go with you". He was the one who brought all my husbands things to me from his apartment.

****

During this process of writing this book so many things have happened and come out about sexual abuse and incest. I went to see the movie "I Can Do Bad All by Myself". Laughing, crying and sobbing through the movie each and every time I watched it, probably ten times. I loved Pastor Wayans, Mary J. Blige, Taraji P. Hanson and especially Gladys Knight. It was like God was sending me the message to keep writing, don't stop.

The songs seemed like they were written for me, especially, "I'm Over It Now". I wanted to name this book, "If I Can Help Somebody"; in the beginning but now I want to name it "I'm Over It Now", if it's ok with Tyler Perry. I keep picturing the book cover with blue skies and clouds, kind of heavenly. They say if you keep picturing something you want in your mind it will happen.

Another book came out written by McKenzie Philips , "High On Arrival"; about her incestious relationship with her father she says was consensual. She was on Oprah and I think she was a very brave woman to come out and talk about her story. Again, I feel like God is telling me now is the time to come out and tell your story, don't be afraid or fear what people will think of you.

I also watched Monique and Oprah talking on her show about the movie, "Precious". Monique also talked about being molested by her older brother. She is a strong, funny, very deep woman and I also get my inspiration from her and Oprah because she has also talked about how she was molested as a child. Monique said there are many younger and older women who have had this happen to them but its such a "taboo" subject that it's often kept secret and swept under the rug, like my story. I haven't seen the movie "Precious" yet but I know it will touch me and inspire me to keep writing. Every Sunday morning I watch "Lift Every Voice" , on BET, this morning Coco said to be like Peter. Step out of the boat on faith, that's what I'm doing.

I finally did go see the movie "Precious" and I had very mixed feelings about it. It was very hard to watch at times because in some parts of it was like watching me. Like Precious in the movie I would take myself away from what was happening to me and imagine I was somewhere else, safe and loved. It's like having an out of body experience where your mind leaves your body and goes somewhere else, it's the only way you can survive it. The one big difference for me is that I didn't have to go through the physical abuse that she did from her mother and she had no one else to show her love. I thank God that I had my Uncles and Aunts, my grandmother, sisters and brothers and cousins that allowed me to experience love, to get love and to give love back.

Chapter Sixteen

College, Arrests, and Juvenile Detention Center

After we had the Memorial Service for my husband and everything quieted down I decided I wanted to go back to College. I had always wanted to be a teacher and since I was now getting social security benefits for my two sons I could go full time and get a Pell Grant. I couldn't believe I was finally going to do something that I had wanted to do for a long time and something for myself. I rented a small house near the college I attended and picked out my classes.

My oldest son was still selling drugs telling himself that he needed to help me financially and I worried about him all the time. I tried to concentrate on school and was in the work study program working in the Dean's office. I tried to be there for my younger sons and asked them to go to grief counseling or family counseling with me but they wouldn't, because we all needed closure.

My youngest son started hanging out with some older boys, staying out very late at night. I didn't know it but he was involved in robbing people's houses. He was finally caught and arrested when he was being the lookout at house they were robbing. His job was to watch outside while the older boys went inside and robbed the house. This particular night the people who lived there came home and surprised them. The husband chased them and the wife called the police. My son was running and fell on some glass and had to have stitches in his hand. They took him to a Juvenile Center because he was only 14 years old.

For two weeks I went there everyday to try and get him out. Again my father surprised me by trying to help, he would go with me to the Juvenile Center, and finally they released him. I began to think my father was sorry for what he had done to his family. When my mother had breast cancer and my sister got very sick he would try his best to take care of them.

My middle son got into the same community college I went to and did well for a while but his girlfriend got pregnant and I became a grandmother to a beautiful baby girl. They didn't stay together long because she had a lot of issues and so did my son. In order to be a good man and father you have to see a good man and father so it was difficult for my sons. My granddaughter was my joy and my son and I had her every week-end, He loved his little girl very much and was a good father which really didn't surprise me since he had told me since a young teenager that he wanted to be a father. He would change diapers, feed her, bathe her, yet he was only twenty years old and still struggling with many issues.

Soon after my grand daughter was born my oldest son got arrested for selling cocaine. We got him a lawyer but his case was serious and he was older, he went away for three years to Attica. Right before he went away he and his girlfriend had a beautiful baby girl also. I remember when he dropped the pregnancy test that was positive in my lap. I was so happy and I thought it might make him stop selling drugs but it didn't work out that way.

His girl and I went to visit him and took the baby to try and keep his spirits up. I loved being a grandmother and I had two beautiful granddaughters. After having three sons it was the best thing I could have ever imagined. I had both of them just about every week-end. While my son was away his girl started to see someone else and when he came home they tried to work on their relationship but it was too late.

For a while he went crazy, threatening and fighting for his family to stay together but she eventually chose the other guy. He couldn't accept it and really wanted to hurt the other man she was with. One day after they argued on the phone he threatened him, got a gun and drove to their house. When he got there his girlfriend's brother was already there because she had called him, afraid of what my son might do.

When my son got out of the car and started to walk towards the house he shot him in the leg. He told me much later that he was so fearful of what might happen it was the only way he knew to stop him. It hurt him to shoot my son because they had been friends since High School but he was afraid my son was going to hurt his sister because he looked so crazed and angry. After my son got shot it was like the bullet had some kind of healing medicine in it. He left his girl and her new boyfriend alone, didn't press charges and started to turn his life around. He got a job in a bowling alley making $7.50 an hour, got himself a studio apartment and met another girl.

After being in that Juvenile Center for two weeks my youngest son went back to High School and graduated, he never got into any trouble again after that. My middle son never got into any trouble with the law, worked and took care of his baby girl on the week-ends. He wouldn't let himself get really involved with another woman saying he just wanted to concentrate on being a Dad. During all of this I managed to continue to go to college, I had pretty good grades and was determined to graduate.

Chapter Seventeen

Murder Confession,
Mom Dies from Cancer

Just when I thought maybe my father was trying to make up for the years if abuse he put his family through he again showed his real true colors. My aunt who lived next door to my mother had a son who had been in and out of jail for just about everything, stealing, dealing drugs, pimping, and his last crime that put him in jail for a long time was kidnapping a young girl and turning her into a prostitute. The young girl just happened to be the daughter of a policeman, they sent him away for thirty years.

While in prison he "found" God and confessed that he had murdered another young girl and buried her. He had killed her in the summer house that was behind my Mom and Dad's house and buried her in the woods behind their house. All of a sudden the FBI, police, and news reporters were swarming all over my parents' house. My father took off to whereabouts unknown and left my mother there to face the music. He was obviously involved somehow, probably had sex with the girl with my cousins ok in the little summer house but didn't know he would kill her for some reason.

The FBI brought him down from prison to show them where he had buried the body and it was exactly where he said it would be. They dug her body up and notified her parents because she was missing for a number of years. My dad disappeared during all of this like I said and left my mother to deal with all of this. We were all ready to kill him when he finally came back but my mother stopped us, especially my brothers who wanted to kick his ass. I really gave up hope on him and didn't want anything to do with him after that and asked my sons to stay away from him too.

My mother's cancer came back when I was in my last semester of college. We knew she was sick again but the doctors couldn't pinpoint where the cancer had returned. By the time they figured out it was in her liver it was too late, we lost her in three months. I dropped out of school for a while to help take care of her. We all took turns taking care of her and spending the night, my sister from California came to help too. We did the best we could not wanting to believe she was going to leave us soon.

They diagnosed her in July and we buried her on her birthday October 24th. My mother and fathers 50th wedding anniversary happened to come on October 1st and we had a party for them in the hospital because my mother had developed a blood infection and was too sick to leave the hospital. We brought her a flower corsage to wear on her hospital gown because she was too weak to even get dressed. We had it catered in one of the large rooms the hospital let us use and my mothers cousins were there, all her children and grandchildren. She tried to look happy but I knew she was in a lot of pain.

I kept wondering to myself what are we celebrating? My mother staying married for 50 years to a man who abused two of her daughters, almost killed one of her sons, beat her, cheated on her, had no respect for our family, Why? The whole celebration was a farce and so were her 50 years of being married to him. I promised her I would take care of my baby sister who was getting sicker and sicker everyday. Her disease was progressing and she couldn't walk anymore. Her spirit was strong and still remains strong to this day.

My father had taken care of my mother, taking her to chemotherapy, fixing special meals she could digest, making carrot and apple juice, even giving her morphine when the doctor knew she was in a lot of pain. He also did the best he could trying to help take care of my baby sister at the same time. My hatred for him started to diminish and I prayed to God to forgive him. They say if you don't forgive someone they still have control over you. You're forgiving the person for yourself not for them. I tried really hard to put the past behind me.

Chapter Eighteen

Relationships In My Life

I finally managed to graduate from college, with an Associates Degree, and I was proud of myself for finishing something I started. I got a job as a Counselor with emotionally disturbed children and planned on finishing school and getting a Bachelor's Degree and becoming a teacher like I planned. During this time I had a few relationships, some good and some bad. They never lasted long because I was not healed, not open for a loving, trusting relationship. Still drawn to men who really didn't love me, had addictions themselves that they were dealing with. I was still addicted to marijuana and smoking every day and spending way too much money.

One man that my older sister introduced me to was very good to me, loving, kind, generous and I wish to this day that I had kept him in my life and married him. He was shorter than me and light skinned as we Black folks would say, even though I've always been attracted to brown skin men. He was kind, generous, and very attentive to me. He took me out all the time to jazz clubs, concerts, one time I'll never forget was to the "Blue Note" to see Phyllis Hyman one of my favorite singers. He worked for IBM and drove a tan Mercedes Benz. He had been married before but was divorced and had a 16 year old daughter.

His father had just passed away when we met so he was living with his mother helping her get over her grief. Their house was huge so there was plenty of room. His mother liked me and we got along great. My sons really liked him too and that was important to me. I let him go for another man who was ten years younger than me, an alcoholic like my father. He was good looking and chocolate brown like Wesley Snipes.

I met him on the bus going to College everyday. We started out as friends because I kept reminding him I was ten years older than him. He would draw pictures for me because he was an excellent artist, then paintings that I loved, then jewelry and giving me flowers often. He finally wore me down and we went out to dinner and a movie. He had been in a bad relationship previously where his girlfriend cheated on him. He had a 6 year old daughter that I liked very much to spend time with. He also lived with his mother who was very nice but also an alcoholic. She had been very badly abused by her husband and left him but had to hide from him for many years out of fear.

He told me many times how his father beat his mother in front of them so he had many issues going on in his life too. We lived together for two years. My sons didn't like him and he eventually cheated on me with a young white girl, PWT (poor white trash) as we Black women would say. I found a letter in his pocket from her, telling him How much she loved him but I didn't say anything. I waited until he went away to his cousins wedding and took his clothes and threw them in the garbage, took his car, took the plates off and parked it in my sister's backyard. When he came back he had no clothes, no car and no place to live. I guess the Scorpio came out in me and like they say its a thin line between love and hate. It was a long time before I wanted anything to do with any man.

Then one day I got a phone call from a guy I went to High School with. He told me he got my phone number from a mutual friend, another guy because we had all hung out in High School together. There weren't that many black kids in my high school in the sixties so we all knew each other. He was a very smart, kind of nerd who was best friends with a guy that I dated in High School. I guess he had a crush on me but never said anything. He was very shy, wore a tie everyday and was our Senior Class President.

He was now a doctor living in Baltimore, said he was divorced and began calling me everyday telling me lies, sending flowers and cards, etc. I fell for all his lies and we began a relationship. I started to believe that maybe God had finally sent a good, decent man into my life. I was so wrong. He was a total liar, a cheater and had not turned out to be a good man at all. I used to pray that something bad would happen to him.

He had the audacity to come to our 20th High School Reunion and I seriously thought of having someone beat him up, maybe break an arm or a leg while he was in town. But I kept hearing God's voice telling me to let him handle it. After those bad episodes with men I locked my heart and haven't let anyone in. I decided I can't love or be loved until I can stop being addicted to marijuana and be healed from this secret I've been hiding all these years.

Chapter Nineteen

Move to Virginia

My youngest son and his girl decided to move to Virginia to try and make a better life for there. It was too expensive on LI so they packed up and moved to Virginia Beach. When I went to visit them I loved it and eventually decided to move there too. I didn't want to leave my other sons and grandchildren but I thought maybe they would come and visit and like it too and move there. My youngest son seemed to be doing good, they had their own apartment and local jobs in the neighborhood.

Little did I know that my son was robbing people's houses with some other guys he had met there. A few months after I moved there he was arrested and went to jail. I didn't have any money to get him a good lawyer like I did with my oldest son. Plus the fact that we were in Virginia, a Commonwealth with laws that dated back to the slave days.

He didn't have any real previous record or a weapon but without a good lawyer they railroaded him and he was sentenced to ten years. I fell to my knees when they read his sentence and couldn't believe my ears. My precious baby boy who wouldn't hurt a fly was going to lose ten years of his life, he didn't kill anyone or hurt anyone, and it just didn't seem fair. I know what he did was wrong, stealing and going into other people's houses but he didn't deserve ten years. I tried to appeal it but his legal aide lawyer was the worst and she could have cared less.

I tried to be there for his girl and my grandson but it wasn't long before she met another guy and started to be with him. Then my baby sister got very sick and started having multiple seizures so I moved back to New York to be closer to her. I got my job back and tried to just live my life and stay positive. I was still smoking marijuana every day, spending money and moving from apartment to apartment .

My other sons were doing well and we went to Virginia often to see my youngest son. My oldest son went back to school and became a Medical Biller and my middle son got a job in a Rehab Center and eventually got custody of his daughter. Her mother was now with another man and had a new baby boy. She made one big mistake when she started working leaving my granddaughter while she worked 3pm to 11pm. The final straw came when her boyfriend sent my granddaughter to bed with no dinner as a punishment. My son went and got his daughter and she has been with us ever since. That was three years ago and she doesn't want to go back and live with her mother. Between my son and I we manage to take care of her and she's happy with us.

My life revolved around my sons and grandchildren and my sister, helping to take care of her the best I can. She has her son and daughter and a beautiful granddaughter and they do the best they can. The truth be told my sister keeps me going, she's such a spirited, strong person, a survivor, and a fighter. She truly is like Sade's song says a "soldier of love" in every way, living, loving doing her best to stay alive.

When I start to feel sorry for myself I look to her or listen to one of her pep talks. I think to myself, she can't walk, sometimes she's in a lot of pain, but she keeps going everyday. What do I have to complain about? I can get up in the morning, I go to a job that I love, and I can bathe myself, comb my hair, and brush my teeth. She can't do any of those things and she lives her life everyday dependent on other people. When I tell her I can't seem to let go of the past and what happened to us, she tells me it wasn't our fault , to let it go and leave the past in the past. I try but I guess we have different spirits because I just can't seem to do it.

Chapter Twenty

I Need Closure and Peace at Last

After my mother died my father left my brother the house and moved to Florida. He comes up to New York from time to time, on holidays or his birthday. On one of his recent visits he told all of us that he was leaving his house in Florida to his 1st male heir, my oldest brother and it's to be shared with my younger brother. He supposedly has left the girls some piece of property in Florida to be shared among the four of us.

My older sister was kind of upset because every time my father has been in a financial bind she has bailed him out and has helped him keep his house and the property. My other sisters and I never really expected anything from him or want anything from him but it was like he was saying women are worthless, he has no respect for us or our mother and we're only good for one thing. I told him he had five beautiful daughters before he had a son and he could keep his property.

Everyone acts like he never did anything and I try to forget what he did to us and to my mother. I never let my grandchildren be around him without me and I have told my sons the same thing. As ironic as it seems my oldest granddaughter has the same birthday as him. My sister that lives in California doesn't have anything to do with him, won't even speak to him.

Recently when my baby sister got very sick and had to have an emergency tracheotomy she started to come around a little, speaking to him and being a little more tolerable. But in reality she's right to not want anything to do with him. He's 83 years old but he's still a no good perverted bastard.

We recently (last summer) had a family reunion with our cousins (my aunt's daughters) and they're children. We haven't bee together for several years. It was great to be together again because when we were younger we were very close. They are my father's nieces, beautiful women all grown up to be strong, independent women in spite of the fact they lost their mother at a very young age. My father decided to take this opportunity to touch my cousin (his niece) on the ass.

He came up behind her while she was bending over getting a soda out of the refrigerator and just put his hand on her ass and felt it like it was nothing. My cousin never told me until they all went back home. I asked her why she didn't say or do anything and she said she didn't want to spoil the reunion. She also has two grown sons and if they found out he did that they would not have let him get away with it. I told her she should have slapped him across the face, and not worried about spoiling the reunion. I felt so bad, embarrassed, and angry again, wanting to call him and curse him out and tell him all the things I've been wanting to say for so long.

But again, my baby sister prayed with me and I just put it in God's hands. I know that my father will burn in hell for what he's done and that's my only consolation. I've told my other sisters and brothers that I don't want anything to do with him anymore and for the first time in my life I'm going to be true to myself.

Writing this book has been a healing experience for me because I haven't smoked any marijuana since the summer. One day I was smoking a joint and I suddenly felt like I was having a heart attack. It was one day when it was 97 degrees and my heart started to pound so loud I could hear it in my ears. I was sitting in my car and I had the air conditioner on full blast but it wasn't helping.

I kept talking to myself trying to calm down but I couldn't and felt like I was going to pass out. I kept praying and I promised God if he helped me calm down I would never smoke again. I started beeping the horn so my son would come and help me into the house. He helped me into the apartment and I got into a cool shower and eventually the anxiety attack stopped. I know in my heart it was God making me stop because I kept praying to him everyday to help me stop smoking marijuana. I haven't smoked since that day and it is now Thanksgiving time, 2009. I want to finish this book before December 24th, my nephew's birthday end give it to him as a birthday present. I want him to be the first one to read it since he is the one that started me on this journey.

I've been stuck or should I say at a standstill trying to finish writing this book. I haven't written anything lately because I've been spending time with one of my best friends because her husband just passed away from cancer. She has been my best friend since high school, was my maid of honor when I got married. She was also the only friend that I confided in and told about the sexual abuse with my father. She and her husband were there for me when my husband died and her husband was always there for my sons when they needed a man to talk, they knew they could always go to him and talk about whatever was bothering them.

He would always listen and then give wise words of advice. My friend and I have been having lots of heart to heart talks about everything that's happened in our lives. She's been through a lot in her life also, losing her mother, having a disabled brother in a state hospital for many years, her baby sisters were both on drugs, yet she still stayed strong and encouraged me to stay strong. I told her about writing this book and how it's helped me to heal but I don't know how to end it. She told me to keep praying and to forgive my father and my husband, not for them but for myself. She said just keep writing and the end will come to you.

Christmas has come and past, New Year's Day when I made my resolutions and now it's February and I can't seem to come up with an ending for my book. I would like to end it with my father's death so I can have some closure but since he is still alive I can't end it like that. Should it be a happy ending with me saying how happy I am and what a good life I have in spite of what happened to me. That would not be the truth even though I am blessed in many ways.

Right now my life is fairly good. I still don't make a lot of money I live in an apartment with my granddaughter. I'm helping my son raise his daughter, she's thirteen ,a typical teen-ager and sometimes a handful but her father is there to help me keep her in line and her mother lives close by also. My middle son is still not married but he's doing good, working at a Rehabilitation Center making pretty good money and is happy just to have his daughter in his life.

I keep asking him when he's going to get married and have another child but he says right now he just wants to concentrate on raising his daughter and he has some "friends " that he enjoys spending time with. I work as a Residential Counselor with emotionally disturbed children and I love what I do. My oldest son is finally working at what he went to school for, medical billing and I'm very proud of him for turning his life around. He and his fiancé just told me they are expecting a baby in July and I'm very excited about being a grandmother again. My son's daughter is nine years old and I see her often, she spends the weekend with me often and is still in that sweet pre-teen age and does whatever I ask her to do.

My youngest son is still in jail in Virginia but will be coming home soon, hopefully by the end of this year. He has made a lot of changes in himself, has completed an auto mechanics job course while there and also taken several college courses. But most importantly has turned to God to help him get through his prison term. His son is seven years old now and I saw him for a while at Christmas but haven't talked to him since then. His mother doesn't really keep in touch with me and doesn't really take my grandson to see his father even though she lives right in Virginia but I just pray on that situation and I know my son will be home soon and I'll be with both of them soon.

I haven't been able to finish my book for a lot of reasons. mainly because I'm worried about my sons not being able to deal with some of the things I've written. About three weeks ago I decided to just be happy that I've healed by writing down all the feelings and secrets that I've been hiding for so many years. I stopped smoking marijuana now for eight months and I feel good and finally at peace not keeping all those feelings bottled up inside me. It is now one week before Easter and I've decided to submit my manuscript. I feel like Easter is the perfect time, it represents coming back to life, new beginnings and when God gave his life for our sins.

My Daily Walk Bible today says "your internal strife has ended at last. Sometimes God redirects your plans. The hardest territory to hand over to God is the heartland of your dreams. How do you respond to the death of a dream? When your most cherished ambition is shattered by an unexpected change of plans, what is your reaction? Do you respond with gratitude (not grumbling) and praise (not pouting). Personal ambition must yield to sovereign direction. Have you committed your dreams and ambitions to God? He may want to approve and confirm them, or he may want to change and refashion them into something you've never dreamed of." If God's plan is for me to publish this book then it will happen, if not and it just stays written in my computer I'll be happy with that too. I have faith that God will make the right choice for me.

I still have no man in my life right now and I guess I'm afraid to get involved with any one. I would like to find someone, to be loved and to love again. I guess I have to wait to see if God has that in his plan for my life. I'm hoping my book will come out soon, hopefully this year and change my life and others for the better.

Chapter 21

My Final Thoughts

II have been trying since the beginning of the year to finalize and submit my manuscript. For some reason I've been procrastinating and worrying about if this is the right time to go ahead with publishing my book. Should I wait until my father passes , so he won 't be face the shame and humiliation of what he did to his daughters and family? But why should I, when he never cared about how he made us feel or how it affected us for our whole lives. Even though despite what we went through all of us are decent, caring people with productive lives. None of us are drug addicts, alcoholics or been to jail. Imagine what we could have been if we had a decent father and childhood.

A few months ago my brother told me that my fathers prostrate cancer was back. They can't do surgery because he is 83 years old, nor can they do radiation treatment or chemotherapy. Their only option is to to make him as comfortable as they can . I didn 't call him for fathers day or send him a card for his birthday in March. Will I regeret this after he is gone, I don't think so I'll finally feel some closure and pray that God will have mercy on his soul.

My sister in California read my book and told me that I sound very mean and unforgiving and that is not like me at all. That I should change some of the parts of the book where I sound unforgiving and that I should talk more about my mother and grandmother's life more as young women and the things that happened to them so people will understand them more. I took her suggestions to heart and did include that in my book because I did love them. For the first time in my life I am at peace with myself not trying to have a relationship with my father. What woman would want to have a relationship with a father who sexually abused you? I felt like I wasn 't normal to seek a relationship with him, I would tell myself to dwell on the good things because after all there were some good things that he did for me and my sons. Did he think I would grow up and forget what he did to me and my sister? Did he think it was okay to violate your own daughers? I'm sure I'll never know the answers because he'll probably pass away without us talking about it just like my mother did.